F195 .S14

A DEBATE

BY THE

PHILALETHIC SOCIETY

OF

ST. LOUIS UNIVERSITY,

ON

Monday, February 21, 1870.

"ARMIS FACUNDIA PRÆSTAT."

ST. LOUIS:
GEORGE KNAPP & CO., PRINTERS AND BINDERS.
1870.

PHILALETHIC HALL, February 28, 1870.

GENTLEMEN:—

Considering the late Celebration of WASHINGTON'S Birthday as both interesting to the public and creditable to the Philalethic Society, we hereby request, pursuant to a resolution unanimously adopted by the Members, a copy of your arguments for publication.

Yours respectfully,

D. D. BURNES,
T. W. McATEE,
F. V. REYBURN.

To Messrs. M. J. McLOUGHLIN
CHAS. M. OGLE,
J. J. YARNALL,
J. A. BLAIR,
L. O. KNAPP.

ST. LOUIS UNIVERSITY, February 29, 1870.

GENTLEMEN:—

In compliance with your request, we herewith furnish you with a copy of our remarks, trusting that an intelligent public—which knows how to discriminate between spoken and written language—will bear in mind, that they were never intended to appear in print.

Respectfully,

M. J. McLOUGHLIN,
L. O. KNAPP,
JNO. J. YARNALL,
CHAS. M. OGLE,
JAS. A. BLAIR.

To Messrs. D. D. BURNES,
T. W. McATEE,
F. V. REYBURN.

DEBATE BY THE PHILALETHIC SOCIETY,

ON THE SUBJECT:

"Ought the National Capital to be Removed to St. Louis?"

INTRODUCTORY REMARKS BY THE CHAIRMAN,

M. J. McLOUGHLIN.

Ladies and Gentlemen:—The members of the Philalethic Society appear before you, eager to do their share in making this evening as pleasant as possible. They have chosen a subject, which occupies, at the present time, a considerable portion of the public attention, and which they hope will prove interesting—"Ought the National Capital to be removed to St. Louis." To prevent repetition, each disputant will confine his remarks to some given point. The first Affirmative will try to prove that the capital ought to be removed to 'the Mississippi Valley. The first Negative will maintain the contrary. The second Affirmative will show that St. Louis is the point in the Valley that should be selected as the seat of the National Government, whilst the second Negative will contend against this selection, on the ground that it would prove injurious rather than beneficial to St. Louis.

First Affirmative.

SPEECH OF MR. JOHN J. YARNALL.

Mr. President and Gentlemen:

So intimate are the relations which the capital of a country bears toward the other parts, that to ignore or disregard them is the certain forerunner of coming ruin. It must be to the rest of the country what the sun is to the universe—the centre, around which the minor orbs revolve. Its warm and genial rays must fall upon every spot throughout the length and breadth of the land, enlivening and invigorating every section alike. It must be metropolitan, that is, located in the seat of wealth and empire—in the very midst of commerce and enterprise. Such evidently was the opinion of the first Fathers of the Republic.

Washington City was chosen capital when the United States had a population of about four millions, and it was chosen for the most potent reason, viz: that it was the most central point, and as such served as the connecting link between the great sectional interests of the country. But *then* and *now* are different; things have changed since the good old days of 1800. Progress has advanced in its rapid march across the continent, uniting ocean with ocean; and instead of one small division of thirteen commonwealths, we have three grand divisions of forty commonwealths; instead of three millions of people, armed in the holy cause of liberty, we have forty millions, engaged in the great cause of civilization and—*money-making*. Nay, more, while some of the Eastern States, and especially those of New England, so far from increasing in population are actually diminishing, the centre and the West are developing so rapidly that at the dawn of the 20th century this great sisterhood of States will unite, by an unbroken band, no less than one hundred millions of people.

The public interests are changed—the seat of empire has been borne from its ancient base to the centre of the country. The same relations do not and cannot exist, between the old capital and the country, now as of yore. Washington City is no longer a favorable location, and the national interests, which cannot succumb to those of a small portion of the country, imperatively demand a change. The greatest cities of the past have fallen victims to the shifting of empire and the march of time, and the little town of Washington may as well prepare to meet the same fate with becoming resignation. "Fuit Ilium" will soon be the fittest motto inscribed on its mouldy ruins. Washington was, but is no more.

Our interests are at stake, and she must be sacrificed on the altar of our country—"the inexorable can have no barrier." The busy hum of national life is scarcely heard in her quiet streets; the irresistible tide of wealth, and power, and energy has passed her by in its course, and she is already falling into a lethean obscurity equalled only by that of Sleepy Hollow—the classical realms of our old acquaintance "Rip." Washington City is not the capital of the nation, but of the Atlantic States. They hold her with an agonizing grasp, and through her seek to rule the nation; they wield the power of the country without a right and to our detriment. Is this fair? Is it worthy of our brethren of the East?

Politicians and statesmen regard a balance of power as essential to the peace of Europe, and as soon as one country exercises an undue influence, the others unite to curb its power, and "plucking the growing feathers from her wing, make her fly an ordinary pitch." Might not, should not, the same policy be pursued in an honest, law-abiding way in our own land? Shall we of the centre and the West build up the crumbling walls of the old departments, without any advantage to ourselves? Certainly we are not well balanced here! The hub of the universe is evidently too far east. No wonder, then, that we have sometimes been moving in an eccentric orbit, and more than once been in danger of striking some straying comet.

Add to this, that Washington is notoriously inconvenient of approach, hemmed in as she is by lofty mountains, and having such wretched connections with the North, West and South. Our representatives, as even Benton foresaw, have to come too far. Those from the Pacific slope have to traverse an entire continent—from ocean to ocean—pass by the seat of empire, through all the wealth and energy of the nation, and, after days of weary traveling, at last alight in a gloomy little retreat on the banks of the Potomac.

But more than all, Washington is ever liable to foreign invasion. It is so situated that defence is almost impracticable, and being near the coast, the enemy can surprise and destroy it before a movement is instituted for its protection. Did not the British sack it and drive the executive and heads of departments before them?—and is not the same scene as likely to be enacted in the future? Let us preclude the possibility of a repetition by a removal of the capital. Washington City has ceased to play her part in the great drama of the nation, and her symbolic eagle is winging his flight to other regions, where he is secure against molestation. Thither must the capital be transplanted—to a location dictated by the voice of nature herself, and which everything conduces to make what it ought to be, the *chief city of the nation.* In that spot where beats the heart of the nation, whence ebbs and flows all vital essence through its arterial courses, there and nowhere else should stand America's capital. Who will deny it? Will he who loves to see a smiling land united in its interests and its strength? No! no! The gloomy spectre, the awful visions of our late battle-fields loom up in the hazy distance and confront him at every pass. Did not the late fratricidal struggle originate because of sectional interests? Destroy these and you remove every cause of dissension. Reduce theory to practice, place the capital in that spot where sectional interests coalesce and become national; avoid extremes—"medio tutissimus ibis." Know ye not the spot whereon the gods so favorably smile? Anticipate ye not the site of the coming capital? Yea, your very hearts have uttered the name, before it has yet passed the trembling lips. Minerva speaks! Obey her call.

We are in the midst of the greatest valley of the world. Hither to its centre flow the wealth and power of the nation. Hither also will advance the governing authority; and, at no distant day, this beautiful labyrinth of inland seas shall be hailed by all peoples and nations, as the imperial centre of the Western Hemisphere. Think you I utter a beautiful fallacy? If so, tell me where is the iron that builds our railroads? Where the coal that feeds our steam-engines and warms our parlors? Where the fruits and grains unrivalled in the world? They are here, and each alone, exclusive of the rest, is a source of wealth to any country. Where so much wealth concentrates, there also must reside the political power of the nation.

Nothing but supineness on our part can prevent or retard the speedy consummation of these wishes. Let our people, then, awake to a sense of their interests and their wants; let them act as becomes them in this matter—a matter which so deeply concerns not only the present generation, but likewise the unborn millions that will live after us.

First Negative.

SPEECH OF MR. JAMES A. BLAIR.

Mr. President and Gentlemen :—Though I rise to speak on the negative of this debate, yet far be it from me to say anything that would in the least tarnish the glory of that great city of unblemished fame, which is justly named the Rome of the West, and which bids fair not only to be the Queen of the Valley, but the pride of the country at large—St. Louis, the home of the majority of the audience gathered around us here to-night. Nay, quite as enthusiastic in my admiration as my opponent, I would almost be ready to admit, as he insinuated, that St. Louis is the centre of the Mississippi Valley—that this Valley is the centre of the United States—and the United States the centre of the whole world. But I cannot allow that therefore the capital should be removed hither.

Has he forgotten the millions upon millions of public treasure which have been expended at Washington, in rearing structures that will rival those of any city on either continent? Were it alleged, that experience had shown these buildings to be unsuited to the purpose, for which they were erected, there would be at least some show of reason for incurring the expense of erecting new ones elsewhere. But, Mr. President, nothing of the kind has ever been advanced. On the contrary, it is universally admitted that whilst, by their grandeur, they are a magnificent ornament, they are at the same time, by their adaptibility, an indispensable convenience to the American Republic. Why, then, should they be left to moulder and decay? What! is our present public debt so light a charge that we can afford to increase its weight? Are we not taxed in free Missouri quite abundantly? Are we not taxed for our schools, taxed for our churches, taxed for the very charities that we establish? And shall we deliberately increase this weight by removing the capital, and adding at least millions to the National debt? The poet says that even

"Kings ought to shear, not skin, their sheep."

Let us then first free our nation of that prodigious debt, which neither you nor I will ever live to see effaced; and then those, who live after we shall have long since mouldered in the tomb, may perhaps take into consideration that which with us is at best a baseless vision.

Why find fault with the present location? True, Washington is not the geographical centre of this Union; but this is not by any means a sufficient reason for removing the capital.

In the first place, our numerous railroads have almost annihilated distance, and made us all neighbors. Why, with the facilities at our disposal, a trip from the Pacific coast to the capital is only an agreeable diversion! and we Westerners should vote to keep it at Washington, were it only to give our Representatives an annual tour, and let them enjoy the luxury of the Pullman or Silver Palace sleeping cars.

In the second place, experience has shown that such a position is not essential. Witness Russia. Though this mighty Empire comprises one-fifth of the whole globe, its seat of government is situated at one extremity of its vast territory, St. Petersburg; and yet time has proved that it is now increasing in wealth and population far more rapidly than when its capital was at the geographical centre, Moscow. Now, why should we expect the case to be different with our country? Is it not true, that our own nation's onward flight to greatness and power has ever been associated, in fact as well as in the popular mind, with the capital at Washington? Surely, no one here present needs to be told that if there be in our land one city more than another, whose memories will stir up the feelings and elicit the admiration of an American, that city is Washington—Washington, the seat of Republican government for the last century, and known over the whole world as the capital of a commonwealth more mighty and powerful, than that of which the Cæsars wore the Imperial crown—Washington, named after him who sleeps in his tomb at Mount Vernon, the home of his childhood, on the banks of the silvery Potomac, and almost in sight of the very spot, from which he guided the ship of state, for the period of eight years.

Similar memories clustered around Imperial Rome—memories of glory and greatness, memories of former struggles and triumphs, memories of her rustic heroes and statesmen; and history tells the result which followed, when the traditions and associations of her past were disregarded. When Constantine, in the hour of misguided zeal, desired to establish another Rome at Byzantium, he not only fell far short of accomplishing his project, but destroyed forever, by one single act, more than he had acquired by the well bought victories of many a gory battle field. For the people naturally looked to Rome as the seat of all national power. None other could take its place. Think not that it was the majestic Pantheon, with its now broken idols and extinguished fires—think not that it was even the material structures of the Coliseum, with its lengthy colonnades and towering arches, that drew the truant heart away from the splendors of the new capital. No! it was the noblest, strongest aspiration of the heart, which it is as difficult to change, as to turn the natural course of a mountain torrent. From that day the Romans were no longer one, and the proud Empire of Quirinus saw her "glories star by star expire," until she was buried in the deepest night.

Such will be the effect in our land, if we attempt to change the capital. For the people have learned to recognize Washington as the place where all national power should reside, and they can never accustom themselves to view another in the same light. The present capital may crumble into dust, the ivy may creep in mazy wildness along its dilapidated columns, the solitary owl may hold her gloomy vigils among its mouldy arches, yet our most distant descendants will turn towards its venerable ruins, to catch the echoes of a Webster's eloquence or a Benton's wisdom, still resounding through its vaults; and, wandering from hall to hall, they will stumble over hallowed recollections, as they near the spot where the heroes once stood, and "tread upon their sacred dust."

But, if the most sacred feelings of the human heart must be sacrificed to the symmetry of appearance, if the nation is going to the enormous expense of removing the capital for the sake of gratifying a mere whim, why not place it in that city, where there will be no contention in the future, as to its centrality? Let it be at once removed to the true centre, at Columbia, Kansas, or Kansas City, Mo.; but let not St. Louis stain her fair reputation by advancing fictitious claims to a distinction, which, as my colleague will show, must eventually prove to be more of a burden than of an honor.

She needs not this adventitious renown, like some of her more ambitious but less favored rivals. She has a higher destiny, a nobler end, than that of being the resort of political demagogues and intriguing politicians. She is to be the great emporium of commerce and manufactories. Her ports are to be crowded with steamboats and ships from all portions of the globe. She has already begun to take the lead, in all the walks of industry. Her star daily grows brighter and more dazzling in the firmament of progress; and its splendor will continue to increase, long after the stars of rival cities will have sunk below the horizon.

> "She was born with greatness;
> She has honors, titles, power within,
> And vain external greatness may contemn."

Second Affirmative.

SPEECH OF MR. L. O. KNAPP.

Mr. President and Members of the Philalethic Society—Ladies and Gentlemen:—In opposition to my colleague's argument, the gentleman who spoke last remarked, that the financial condition of the country does not justify the expense of removing the capital. Gentlemen, we do not propose to move the capital in *five minutes, or one hour, or one year;* nor do we propose to rebuild the crumbling walls of the *old capital.* But our motto is FESTINA LENTE, and with this will we triumph. We will build one department at a time, and by degrees we will soon erect a capital that shall surpass, in beauty and magnificence, anything that has ever existed.

As my colleague has remarked, that the capital *must* be removed, and that it will eventually be located in the Mississippi Valley, the question now arises: Where in the valley shall we place this mighty bulwark of a nation? Out of the many cities that have applied for this grand governmental prize, upon which should the voice of the nation decide? This, Ladies and Gentlemen, is the question which devolves on me to answer; and although at first glance it may seem quite difficult, yet, when examined attentively, there is scarce a shadow of doubt as to the place, which destiny has marked out as the future capital of our Great Republic "and of the civilization of the Western Continent." Gentlemen, shall I tell you which it is? Is it possible that among an audience like this—composed of so much learning, so much wealth, and so much influence—there is none, save myself, a mere student in a university, who is able to point out the future capital of Columbia? No, I know your feelings too well, to misjudge you in this manner. Were I to call for your vote at the present moment, I am sure the whole assembly would arise and exclaim with a unanimous voice, "*St. Louis and St. Louis alone is the place, destined by Providence to be the future Rome of America—the Babylon of Columbia.*"

The day is not far distant. The West is becoming too powerful for the East; for, as has been well said, civilization is moving westward, and, like the ostrich in its flight, throws sand upon everything behind her; and, before many cycles shall have completed their rounds, sentimental pilgrims from the humming cities of the Pacific coast will be seen where Boston, Philadelphia and New York now stand, viewing, in moonlight contemplations with the melancholy owl, traces of the Athens, the Carthage and the Babel of the Western Hemisphere.

One hundred and six years ago, St. Louis was but an obscure settlement, not even marked on the maps; but in the words of the Irish poet, a little altered,

Westward the star of empire HAS TAKEN ITS WAY ;

and now, where once stood the trading post of Pierre Laclede Liguest, stands St. Louis, the great emporium of the West, and the Queen of the Mississippi Valley. In her onward march, St. Louis has never lost ground. Even while the epidemics of '49 and '66 raged in all their fury, immigrants from all parts of the world were daily arriving in our city, as if to supply the places vacated by the dying; and thus it has ever been, that, even during the most trying moments, *her guardian angel, her patron saint,* THE GREAT ST. LOUIS, has never deserted her; and now, in her 106th year, she claims a population of 265,000 souls.

A magnet is always judged by the force of its attraction, and the power it has of retaining its magnetic influence; and thus do I judge St. Louis. Not only does she attract, but, as I have shown, she retains; and, gentlemen, those now living may see the day, and not far off, when St. Louis, the great magnet of the Western hemisphere, will contain a population of no less than 1,000,000 persons.

In regard to wealth, there is not a city in the Union, of the same age and size, that is able to cope with St. Louis. Even Chicago, with her immense Eastern capital, after exhausting millions in her attempt to create a crisis in our city, has given up all hopes, and is now advocating in favor of St. Louis.

This great wealth is owing to our inexhaustible commercial facilities; we are, as it were, the great commercial centre of the Republic, the storehouse from which is drawn the material, that furnishes not only the manufactories of America, but also, to a great extent, those of foreign countries. St. Louis is not only situated within a few miles (500) ride from the geographical centre, but it is the undoubted commercial centre. Its radii, composed of rivers and railroads, like the rays of the sun, point to all parts of the universe, and, go where you will, even to the barbarian shores of Asia and Africa, and you will find the footprints of our agents who have been there before you.

A few years ago, one of our greatest statesmen, in a speech to the United States Senate, was laughed at for saying: "*There is the East —there is India.*" Who among us to-night would dare, on his peril, make light of these words? If there be any such, let them beware, lest the spirit of Thomas H. Benton arise and brand them with the curse of insanity. The prophetic words of Mr. Benton have been realized. INDIA IS THERE, AND WE HAVE FOUND IT. Some (among them, the gentleman who spoke last) have rashly asserted that, in a business point of view, St. Louis will be ruined if placed under a Con-

U of M

gressional rule; that this will drive away commerce, decrease the value of property, and, in a word, make it a city of money-made aristocrats, who stay at home and make a living off the interest of their bonds. These, Ladies and Gentlemen, are groundless suppositions. Those who advance them have no arguments to prove their assertions. They are but affirming a consequent without an antecedent, proclaiming an effect without a cause, and therefore they utter words like an automaton, ignorant of their meaning. For instance, the assertion made by the gentleman who spoke last, "that neither you nor I would live to see the present national debt erased." This I will treat with silence; for we all know that we are not now being taxed for the benefit of the government, to raise revenue, or to pay our national debt. No, Ladies and Gentlemen, America, thank God, is not yet a *bankrupt.* She has money enough in her coffers, to pay her debt in thirty days, if called upon. Why, in one year, the surplus proceeds of the Valley alone would pay the national debt.

To return to the first point. Tell me *one*—one single capital of so great a power as this, that has not flourished. History, as far as the days when commerce was in its infancy, fails to mention a single city that had lost its power and influence on account of its being a capital. Washington itself, although situated in so unfavorable a position, has not been declining. This, Ladies and Gentlemen, is an excellent example; for by it we see that a city, without any resources in a commercial line, has not lost anything, but, on the contrary, we see that it owes what little importance it has to the fact of its being the capital. But situated in so unfavorable a position, it is impossible for it ever to become a great city; and to this same infelicitous position is due the fact of its now being, as is evident, little better than a disgrace to the nation which it represents. But, as my colleague has already remarked, "its death day is come;" for the people are awakened to a real sense of the necessity of a change, and they are determined, that the greatest power of the globe shall also have the greatest capital. Where it shall be, remains to be seen. All we can assert at present is, that the city, which has the most promising position in regard to wealth and commercial facilities, shall also have the honor of being the representative of the country, whose father's anniversary we celebrate to-night. There are a few cities in the Union now far ahead of St. Louis; but there is not a city in the whole United States, much less in the Mississippi Valley, that has better or more promising prospects than St. Louis. But, as my colleague has already proved that the capital must come to the valley, and as the last gentleman has admitted that it should be placed in the most favorable position if moved at all, I claim St. Louis as the place. For I have shown that, in spite of all difficulties and adversity, she has constantly advanced in population, improved in wealth and commerce, and is now ranked among the first marts of the world. I do not call on the mystic heralds of futurity to prove my assertions. nor do I claim consequences without reasons; but with the United States map in one hand, and the government statistics in the other, with the light of history to guide me on my path, I have steered safely through the breakers, and proved from actual figures, that there is not a more promising city in the Union than St. Louis.

Hence, considering that the capital of a nation is, or at least ought to be, a city of importance in the world, I claim that our own sweet home has preëminent claims over all competitors to be the capital of the Union, as she is now the Queen of the Mississippi Valley.

Second Negative.

SPEECH OF MR. CHARLES M. OGLE.

Mr. President and Gentlemen:—Judging from the speeches of my honorable opponents, one would suppose that they are seriously afflicted with what Dr. Johnson might have called the "cacoëthes regnandi"—as if it were the greatest thing on earth to legislate for others—"triumphatis dare jura Medis!" Now, however great the glory which must always follow the capital of our country, it can never compensate St. Louis for the advantages that she would at once be obliged to forego, were she selected for the envied dignity.

Shall we, then, who after so many years of unbounded anxiety and toil have reared our city to a degree of unrivalled perfection, allow the interests most dear to us to be sacrificed and become subservient to those of the General Government? Yet, Gentlemen, I assure you this will inevitably be the result, if the Capital be removed hither. We shall lose those who have so brilliantly adorned and upheld our city, and who from the seat of administration have defended the rights of the nation, and in a particular manner the claims of our own people; in a word, we shall be impoverishing ourselves to enrich all the other portions of the country.

Remember, Gentlemen, the honor that has been gained for our State and city, by the efforts of that illustrious personage, whose name is still fresh in your memories, and who, for thirty long years in the United States Senate, guarded with the interest of a parent the prosperity of the Western country, and especially the advancement of his own beloved home, St. Louis—whose image is now ornamenting our magnificent park, and gazed upon as an emblem of immortal fame. Perhaps there are some in our midst to-day who, in time, would be crowned with the same glory, but whom, by adopting the course which you so earnestly vindicate, we shall be compelled to sacrifice.

For, the capital is the only portion of the country not-represented; strangers govern it and live upon its very substance. If you remove it hither, we shall be submissive to the wishes of those whom we know not, and who, regardless of our own improvement, will devote their energies to promote the interests of their respective States. What matters it to them, whether the city in which they hold their session thrives or not, provided they can satisfy their constituents? What will prompt the Senator from a rival State to favor our grain trade movement, or the completion of the bridge, when he is fully instructed by his constituents to allow no one to come in competition with their pretended claims? Chicago knows this full well and cunningly favors the removal to St. Louis. Her generosity is so unprecedented and so thoroughly unselfish, that we would almost feel like returning the compliment, had she even the faintest claim to such a distinction. Perhaps it might add to her glory; it certainly cannot add to ours.

If our city is destined to be the capital of the United States, that commerce, which is now our pride and our boast, will at once decrease; the majestic steamers, which traverse the Mississippi and daily throng our wharfs for the purpose of transporting our merchandise, will no longer seek for a harbor on our shores, but, to our great astonishment and regret, will perchance resort to that insignificant borough on the opposite shore, East St. Louis—which will then have outrivalled us in commerce, and be able to gaze upon us in a spirit of derision and triumph, that will but too plainly make us conscious of the folly of our choice. Outdone by cities that are now so far inferior to us, we shall no longer be able to support those who depend upon commerce for their livelihood.

Our enterprising business men will remove to other cities, and the remaining populace will devote their whole attention to political affairs and to other more ignoble professions. Who does not see that a poison, thus slowly instilled into the veins, will by degrees induce a general languor, that must eventually prove fatal to the growth of our city, and, by decimating her now healthy population, degrade her from her queenly pre-eminence to the level of a second rate town?

The vacancy, caused by the departure of most worthy citizens, will perhaps in a manner be filled, by the floating population of Washington city But think you, that this populace will sustain the character of our departed friends? Think you, that such an inundation will be productive of good results? A river suddenly swollen bears along with it the filth and impurities from its shores, and rapidly sweeping over its banks destroys the magnificent structures that it meets in its headlong course, until all the country around bears traces of its ravages. What then would happen, were Heaven to allow the ever-increasing flood of office-hunters and hangers-on to pour into our city? Can you see nothing but Santa Clauses, loaded with blessings and presents, in those strolling characters known by the ludicrous appellation of "Carpet-Baggers"?—nothing but patterns of honesty, in the members of the "gold ring"?—nothing but guardians of virtue, in those nameless beings that gather as instinctively in the present capital as vultures around carrion? If, in addition to this, the officials of the nation, overcome by the greater luxury and the stronger temptations of a large city, should at some future day forget the virtuous examples of their first predecessors, and, imitating the profligate "Patres Conscripti" of declining Rome, should sanction crime by the authority of a great name, St. Louis might as well disown her title of Rome of the West, unless you mean "Pagan Rome," with Vice set up and adored again in her new Pantheon.

Is there no danger, moreover, that this motley population will seriously compromise the peace of our city? If even in Washington, which numbers but a few thousand inhabitants, any striking event—such as the tragic fate that closed the career of a late chief magistrate—causes a general commotion, what would happen in St. Louis, which counts its citizens by hundreds of thousands? The capital of a Republic of necessity contains within itself the elements of a fearful conflagration. It needs but a small spark to set the whole into a blaze.

An interesting political question, taken up in Congress, is enough to kindle the fire, studiously fanned by a favorite leader. Paris, and the reign of terror, afford us a wholesome lesson, by which St. Louis ought to profit. A great city never has been and never can be the capital of a republic, without being exposed to outbreaks, similar to those that occurred in the French metropolis under popular rule.

If, then, we value the independence of our citizens, if we value the prosperity of our commerce, if we value the character of St. Louis, let us not take any steps towards moving the capital hither. If it must be located in this neighborhood, let it be in some little country town, like St. Genevieve, St. Charles, or even Florissant—anywhere but St. Louis. As these places are like so many outposts of our own city, we could not fail to take a special interest in any one of them, that would enjoy the honor of being the capital of the nation. We might even volunteer to fit up hotels with suitable accommodations for the representatives of the people, and set the streets with Nicolson pavement, of which the little village on the Potomac has possibly not yet heard.

As for ourselves, let us shun the incubus, and modestly decline in favor of any other aspirant, content with the honor of having been declared most worthy of the coveted distinction, *by the voice of the country at large.*

CONCLUDING REMARKS BY THE CHAIRMAN,

M. J. McLOUGHLIN.

Ladies and Gentlemen:—In the weekly debates of the Philalethic Society it is customary for the presiding officer to give a decision—a decision in favor of that side which, in his opinion, is sustained by the weightier arguments. But there are times, when the arguments on both sides appear so evenly balanced, that neither seems to have the advantage; and, in such cases, he is compelled, in fairness, to give no decision, or in other words to pronounce the debate a tie. I find myself in that predicament this evening. Both parties have advanced reasons, apparently incontrovertible; and, judging from the applause bestowed upon all the disputants, the audience itself is divided in its opinion. This being the case, I am sure that the gentlemen who participated in the debate will be well satisfied, in leaving the decision to those, who have so kindly manifested their appreciation of the efforts made by the debaters on either side. But, whether St. Louis become the national capital or not, not a doubt can be entertained as to her future prosperity and power.

Nearly a century ago it was said, by one of America's most gifted and eloquent sons, that he could judge of the future only by the past. That saying embodies a truth not less applicable now than it was then.

We can indeed judge of the future only by the past. But, judging by the past, have we not every reason to predict a brilliant future for St. Louis? Are we not justified in asserting that she bids fair to rival, if not surpass, the mightiest cities of ancient or modern times? Examine the past of St. Louis and judge of her future. Look into *her history*—yes, her history, short though it be, but oh, how strange and eventful—

and there read the story of her greatness. Or rather, ask some of those gray-haired men, who sit in this hall to-night, the living witnesses of her wondrous increase. Question them on her past, and they will tell you that they well remember the time when St. Louis was but a quiet village, calmly reposing on the banks of the dark and solemn waters that flow down by her side—a spot barely discernible on the verge of civilization—an outpost, obscure and almost unknown, in that far West, of whose coming greatness few had scarcely dreamed. They will tell you that no steamboats plied up and down the Mississippi—that no locomotives had penetrated through the surrounding wilderness. They will tell you that they knew of no lightning obedient to any power, save the power of Him that rules the storm.

In those days every St. Louisan was well acquainted with the person, prospects, resources and character of every one in the village. But these things gradually changed. First came one group of settlers, then another and another. And they continued to come, and to grow larger and more numerous, until the old men of the *village that was* began to realize the fact, that *they didn't know everybody in St. Louis* any more. Old customs made way for new ones. Steamboats, and locomotives, and telegraph wires, and telegraph offices ceased to be novelties. On every side were to be seen the indications of the city's future greatness. Everything appeared to go by steam; in fact, so rapidly did the city increase, that it appeared to grow by steam. The spirit of progress had descended upon St. Louis, and lo! she stood forth transformed—acknowledged to be what she now is and must ever continue to be, the glorious Queen of the West!

This is the record of St. Louis for the past fifty years; and surely it is a record of which she may well be proud. Her success, too, is all the more flattering, that it has been obtained by the aid of no adventitious circumstances. What she is, that she has become by the force of advantages of which nature herself is the guarantee. Her unrivalled position, her commercial facilities, her agricultural and mineral resources—all these, as has been shown in the course of the debate, are the sources whence St. Louis derives her power. Thus far many of her resources have scarcely been called into requisition, and others are only in process of development.

If, under these circumstances, St. Louis has attained her present wealth and position, is it not fair, is it not reasonable to conclude, that she is destined to achieve a greatness, unsurpassed by any city of this or any other age? What element of greatness had Tyre, Carthage, or Palmyra, that St. Louis does not possess? Had they agriculture? Had they manufactures? Had they commerce? St. Louis combines these three great departments of human industry. She has what they had not—the benefits of civilization the most refined the world ever saw, the assistance of all those marvellous improvements and discoveries in the arts and sciences, which have immortalized the last hundred years, and by the side of which the most brilliant achievements of antiquity dwindle into comparative insignificance.

With such facts as these before our eyes—facts taken from the domain of history and experience—we need no longer dwell upon the indications of the future greatness of St. Louis, but indulge in the brightest anticipations of her coming career.

Yet prodigal as nature has been of her gifts, in order that this city may reap the full benefit of her favors, it is necessary that the people of St. Louis should do all in their power, to develop the resources so lavishly conferred. It is not sufficient that they be mere passive spectators of the efforts made by an energetic few; they must be real, earnest, strenuous workers, veritable "Conditores urbis,"—men determined, energetic, sagacious and persevering, who are actuated by no petty, no unworthy motives, but who are fully impressed with the dignity and the grandeur of the mission they are called upon to fulfil—men who will lay broad and deep the foundation, from which may arise a metropolis worthy to be called the pride of the Great American Republic—the masterpiece of the nineteenth century.

That St. Louis has had such citizens, the names of BENTON, AMES, MULLANPHY, and O'FALLON, abundantly testify. That she still boasts of men, not less public-spirited nor less interested in her welfare, is equally true. But their example must be imitated. As the great English Admiral, Lord Nelson, when about to achieve the most glorious of his victories—wishing to animate his followers—anxious to infuse into *their souls* a portion of that patriotic fire which burned so brightly within his own—hoisted that never to be forgotten signal, "England expects every man to do his duty," so these men, animated by an undying love for St. Louis, and speaking in her name, more by their actions than by words, exclaim, "St. Louis expects every man to do his duty!"

This is indeed the spirit that ought to glow within the breast of every St. Louisan. Then, in the coming time, when those wild western prairies, which as yet have never felt the touch of ploughshare, shall have yielded to the force of man's magic, and have been transformed into smiling fields, teeming with the fruits of civilized labor; when flourishing cities shall occupy those places, where there is now nought save solitude; when songs of Christian praise and thanksgiving shall arise from thousands of temples, in concert with the warblings of the winged tribe; when, in a word, the hum and the bustle of civilized millions shall have succeeded to the solemn loneliness—the appalling stillness of the untraveled and unexplored wilds—then, then St. Louis will be, as a gentleman intimated this evening, the radiating centre, the grand focus, whose rays refulgent with a civilization more perfect than ours, shall penetrate into every quarter of the Republic.

Then, indeed, will the prophesy of Benton be verified: "St. Louis shall be the continental cross-roads." Those iron rails, that now stretch from sea to sea, shall be intersected here by others, reaching from Hudson's Bay to the Gulf of Mexico. These shall be the great avenues, the highways of the nation, to which all other ways shall be but as by-paths. These are the sinews with which St. Louis intends to grapple to herself the wealth and the power, not of this continent alone, but also of Asia. *Nature* has given to her the rod of empire, and *art* will give her the strength to keep it. Here, here, in our midst, beats the heart of the nation even now; its throbbings, faint though they be, are yet distinctly perceptible; but the time will soon be upon us, when every pulsation will be felt throughout the length and breadth of the land.

This, Ladies and Gentlemen, is the destiny of St. Louis—this the mission she is fated to accomplish. And who is there here to-night, that does not wish her *God-speed* in its fulfilment? Who is there that does

not join with me in the heart-felt wish, that when a century hence to-night the moon looks down upon the American continent—when she smiles upon the venerable Father of Waters, old and ceaseless as Time itself—when she silvers with her benignant ray the thousands of heaven-pointing spires, which shall adorn our city—she may behold its people, with hearts as light and as happy as ours, celebrating, like us, the anniversary of Washington's birthday.

A BRIEF ACCOUNT OF THE PHILALETHIC SOCIETY.

The object of this Society is to accustom its members to speak in public, and to furnish them with useful information on topics of general interest.

The President is appointed by the President of the University, and invested with the authority of the Faculty, which he represents; the other officers are elected by ballot.

It was founded in 1832, under the Presidency of the Very Rev. P. J. Verhaegen, S. J. The students of the First Class met in November of the same year, and, after drawing up a Constitution and By-laws, proceeded to organize, with the following result:

RIGHT REV. JAMES VANDEVELDE, *President.*
MR. FREMONT DU BOUFFAY, *Vice-President.*
" P. A. WALSH, *Secretary.*
" THOMAS M. TAYLOR, *Treasurer.*

The following is the order of the succeeding Presidents and Vice-Presidents:

PRESIDENTS.	VICE-PRESIDENTS.
Bernard McGowan.	P. McLoughlin.
Very Rev. P. J. Verhaegen.	Jeremiah Langton, Esq.
Rev. J. A. Sweevelt.	Theophilus Littel.
Right Rev. Geo. A. Carrell.	Col. H. B. Kelly.
Rev. F. P. O'Loghlen.	Hon. Richard Barret.
Edward Q. Waldron.	D. H. Guyon.
Rev. F. B. Jamison.	C. F. Lott.
J. D. Johnson.	Lucien Carr.
Rev. C. F. Smarius.	Thomas Harvey.
Rev. F. X. Wippern.	Homere Mille.
Rev. Wm. Mearns.	Rev. Edward Fitzpatrick.
Rev. J. A. Fastre.	Francis Desloge.
Rev. F. P. Garesche.	Adolphe Menard.
Rev. J. M. J. Converse.	H. B. Murphy.
John Lesperance.	B. M. Chambers.
Rev. John F. X. Tehan.	Adolphe Webre.
Rev. John McGill.	J. M. Verdenal.
Rev. Francis Nussbaum.	B. M. Rice.
R. J. Meyer.	Francis LaMotte, Esq.
	A. J. Kennedy, Esq.
	Santiago Belden.
	Holdridge Collins, Esq.
	Wolsey Collins, Esq.
	Thomas Musgrave.
	Robert Holloway.

The Society possesses a spacious hall, which has been neatly furnished during the course of the present year, and is destined to be still further improved.

On leaving the University, the members are entitled to a Certificate of honorary membership. Any other person, whom the President and the Society deem worthy of special consideration, may share the same privilege.

MOU

The following are the names of the active members now composing the Society:

MR. R. J. MEYER, S. J., *President.*
" M. J. McLOUGHLIN, *Vice-President.*
" D. D. BURNES, *Secretary.*
" LEIGH O. KNAPP, *Treasurer.*
" CHARLES M. OGLE, *First Censor.*
" ROBERT BREARD, *Second Censor.*

MR. LOUIS R. BERGERON.
" J. J. YARNALL.
" F. VALLE REYBURN.
" JOHN BREARD.
" TYLER W. MCATEE.
" JOS. MONTEDONICO.
" ELEUTHERIO BACA.
" EDWARD GLEESON.
" FRANCIS WRIGHT.

MR. JAS. A. BLAIR.
" JOSEPH WEBER.
" CALENDER LEWIS.
" CHARLES LAFORGE.
" STEPHEN MENARD.
" GEORGE WILKINSON.
" TENNILLE MCENERY.
" WM. PROVENCHERE.

The following is a list of those who were formerly active members:

John Walker.
Laurent Segur.
Daniel Hickey.
Louis Laroque.
John Duralde.
Wm. Hardey.
Achile Segur.
Benjamin Soulard.
José Puchey Bea.
J. W. Scarret.
Benj. Eaton.
O. A. Ogden.
W. J. Furguson.
Gustavus Billon,
Edward V. Deroin.
S Simpson.
Alonzo Manning.
John Posey.
Theo. Littel.
Flavius Thompson.
D. G. Rejon.
Ferd. Mudd.
Wm. C. Taylor.
Oscar W. Collet.
Louis Lombard.
Rev. John Verdin.
Peter Poursine.
Jules Sompayrac.
John Morgan.
Wm. Guilmartin.
Landy Delouche.
Rev. George Watson.
Louis Carneal.
Rev. G. H. Kernion.
Francis Roubien.
F. L. Garesché.
F. P. Leavenworth.
Chas. F. Lott, Jr.
Wm. T. Coleman.
H. B. Brant.
G. C. Hartt.
J. S. B. Alleyne, M.D.
J. B. Graham.
E. F. Smith, M.D.
Nathan Rannels.
B. W. Lott

Jos. W. Walsh.
James Walsh.
J. J. Anderson.
Samuel McGill.
John Shannon.
Robert Reilly.
Wm. Kinney.
John Klein.
Justin Landry.
J. Michel.
Joseph Larguier.
J. Haggerty.
J. LaFaye.
Chas. Kennedy.
L. Texada.
Russel Curtis.
Robt. Beamon.
Alfred Thorington.
Wm. Moore.
Manuel Regil.
Manuel Medina.
James Halligan.
A. Mendes.
Peyton Spence.
Wm. Romeyn.
Andrew Murphy.
Joseph Verdin.
W. M. McNair.
Valière Dupuy.
Joseph Hall.
Theo. LaVeille.
A. H. Kernion.
Col. H. B. Kelly.
Calhoun Benham.
Alex. Garesché, LL.D.
Chas. Childs.
Geo. Graham.
Arthur Gallagher.
H. P. Shurburne.
P. M. Blair.
V. Carr Lane.
Allen W. Davy.
E. E. Curtis.
Chas. B. Smith.
Wm. H. McGuire.
Jas. J. McBride.

Eugene Swindler.
Augustus Roche.
George Simpson.
Silvère Deloche.
Benj. Fonteneau.
P. Corlis.
Valsin Dupuy.
Sylvester Papin.
P. Bludworth.
Thos. O'Connel.
Chauve Labeaume.
Lucien Roubien.
Theophilus Commagère.
Severin Trichel.
Armand Boissat.
Chas. Tessier.
Edward Carr.
Samuel Stewart.
Edw. Jennings.
Wm. Alexander.
Lucien Trichel.
Thomas Watson.
G. McKeever.
J. E. Darst.
Theodosius Barret.
Hon. Richard Barret.
I. N. M. Harding.
Benjamin Farrar.
A. K. McLean.
Rev. Thos. O'Neil.
E. C. Winchester.
Rev. F. P. Garesché.
D. W. Sheppard, Esq.
F. E. Relly.
Rev. T. M. Finney.
Jas. W. Davis.
Jno. Q. Burbridge.
R. F. Miller.
Francis Duplissis.
Guyton Jones.
Jas. R. Larkin.
Henry Von Phul.
John Yore.
Byron Kirby.
Henry Chouteau.
Jas. Rotchford.

Lucien Carr.
Guyen Tompkins.
P. Donnelly.
Alex. McGuire.
Marco Givanovich.
Bernard Farrar.
M. Hayes.
Edward Morehead, M.D.
Edward Lynd.
Louis Leduc.
Jer. F. Young.
Jas. A. Kennedy, Esq.
Francis Desloge.
A. Menard.
J. A. Bienvenu.
H. B. Murphy.
H. G. Soulard.
C. P. McCune.
J. D. Galvin.
R. V. Corcoran, Esq.
Overton Barret.
Adolphe Webre.
Geo. Dickinson.
Edw. McCabe, Esq.
Chas. Conwell.
Gilman Chouteau.
Wm. Shaw.
Wm. C. Crone.
Sol. W. Steigers, M.D.
R. W. Anderson.
Jos. McNeil.
Rev. P. O'Reilly.
Thos. J. Drum.
Bernard Gautier.
J. A. Davenport.
F. X. McCabe, Esq.
Fr. X. LaMotte, Esq.
Wm. J. Rickert, Esq.
J. T. Wilson.
L. J. Ducoté.
A. G. Hawes.
Wm. J. Corkery.
Jno. P. Hogan.
Jno. De Brees.
Jules Desloge.
Jer. F. Conroy, Esq.
W. S. Pratt.
W. A. Morris.
Chas. H. Chenot.
Chas. LaMotte.
Peter Corcoran.
W. A. Bickford.
Thos. H. Trigg.
L. J. Cella.
Hiram F. X. Fairbanks.
Chas. F. Loker.
John P. Donaher.
Jno. McCallum.
C. B. Eaton.
T. J. Smith.
F. A. Jones.
J. M. Worthington.
Edw. W. Wallin.
J. W. Golden.
J. M. Wolbrecht.
Jno. C. Powell.
J. F. R. McEnnis.
Leon J. Papin.
Adolphe Brazene.
Isaac J. Cooper.
E. Forstall.
Paul Poincy.
Edm. H. Trépagnier.
Homère Mille.
Wm. Linton.
F. N. Trépagnier.
Victor Pujos.
Leon Webre.
J. L. Vincent.
Chas. H. Harber.
Geo. J. Hood.
B. M. Chambers.
Jno. H. Reel.
J. J. Ducoté.
J. D Finney.
Jas. J. Finney.
Jas. J. Sweeny.
Jas. A. Kelly.
Matthew Johnson.
Theodule Camus.
Thos. Dorris.
Augustus Ewing.
Jno. Verdenal.
Geo. Douglas Ramsay, Jr.
J. Diller Ruth.
Jno. J. Quinlan.
Julius S. Walsh.
Bernard Rice.
S. B. Pallen.
M. M. Boissac.
Jas. F. Byrne.
Hugh A. Boyle.
Jas. H. Yore.
Thos. Hurst.
Louis S. Tesson, M.D.
Jno. Moynihan.
Jas. A. Beatty.
John J. Quealy.
Jno. J. Rodgers.
Santiago Belden.
G. W. Fichtenkam.
Lloyd Mitchell.
J. S. Mauntel.
F. J. Donovan.
Wm. L. Loker.
G. S. Berthold.
W. J. Pickett, Jr.
Lewis C. Smith, Esq.
Bernard Finney.
Shep. Barclay, Esq.
James Budd.
David Dunphy.
Jno. Braidy.
R. T. Holloway.
E. F. Aehle.
M. C. Lynch.
Eugene M. Morrison.
D. E. Brittenum.
Leon Greneaux.
Thos. H. Musgrave.
Chas. Delhommer.
Jas. O'Neil.
E. J. Carrel.
A. R. McCrummen.
Wm. F. Whelan.
Edgar Pitot.
John Lesperance.
Jos. Wright.
Patrick Carolin.
Chas. Leaumont.
Edw. T. Farish, Esq.
Montrose Pallen, M.D.
John Ainslie.
Wm. I. Kenny, Esq.
Am. Gautier.
Rev. T. B. Chambers.
Geo. Wise.
Edward Leavy.
Rev. F. M. Keilty.
J. P. Murphy.
Augustus Verret.
Nap. R. Hemkins.
H. Clay Hay.
Francis Hood.
Bernard Brady.
Charles Wise.
David McKernan.
R. J. Meyer.
Bryan Clemens.
F. X. Marsot.
Jno. O'Connor.
Eugene H. Brady.
Levi Davis.
D. F. Verdenal.
John Langton.
A. J. Kennedy, Esq.
J. A. Ketterer.
Henry A. Munks.
Gerald L. Griffin, Esq.
Césaire Lemoine.
Jno. Austin Walsh.
Geo. Loker.
Jno. A. Walsh.
Thos. G Brent.
L. V. Cartan.
Jno. A. Woodson.
Edm. G. Pallen.
N. O. Champagne.
Holdridge Collins, Esq.
F. L. Weinman.
Jas. Butler, Esq.
Duncan McCallum.
W. W. Collins, Esq.
Patrick Murphy.
John O'Meara.
T. Aloysius Howard.
Michael Flood.
Chas. Fanning.
Chas. Budd.
J. M. Hertzog.
J. C. Scull.
Edw. F. Haydon.
Wm. L. Trowbridge.
G. H. Backer.
Sam'l Worthington.

G. W. Wallin.
Wm. P. Lynch.
M. Cushing.
John Halpin.
Isaac Taylor.
Wm. H. Haws.
M. S. McCallum.
Ferd. T. Bates.
M. J. Doherty.
M. Wm. O'Neil.
John Kennedy.
Thos. S. Fitzgerald.
Wm. M. Smith.
Geo. W. Waite.
J. O. Ming.
Roger Herring.

The following have been elected honorary members, and have acknowledged their affiliation by letters preserved in the archives of the Society :

Hon. Wm. Carr Lane.
Hon. Wilson Primm.
A. B. Chambers, Esq.
J. C. Dinnies, Esq.
Hon. Bryan Mullanphy.
C. P. Chouteau, Jr., Esq.
Dr. Orestes A. Brownson.
J. V. Huntington.
Robert Bakewell, Esq.
Very Rev. P. J. Ryan.
S. McLean, Esq.
H. A. Prout, M.D.
Hon. R. M. Johnson.
Hon. Martin Van Buren.
Hon. Daniel Webster.
Randolph Rouand, M.D.
Pierce C. Grace, Esq.
Hon. E. A. Hannegan.
Felix McArdle.
Hon. H. J. Spaunhorst.
Hon. L. E. Lawless.
Hardage Lane, M.D.
Edmund McCabe, M.D.
V. M. Garesché, Esq.
B. B. Brown, M.D.
Hon. Henry Clay.
Hon. L. M. Kennett.
Thos. C. Reynolds.
Hon. L. V. Bogy.

www.ingramcontent.com/pod-product-compliance
Lightning Source LLC
LaVergne TN
LVHW020634110826
845149LV00004B/1184

9781418190934